Unfolding How to Use iPad Pro 2020

A Complete Instruction and Practical Guide to Maximizing
iPad Pro 2020

ROBERT

WILLIAM

Copyright

Printed in the United States of America

©2020 by Robert William

Contents

Chapter Six 58

Settings 58

Chapter Seven 87

Troubleshooting Common Problems.... 87

Why This Guide?

With the release of iPad Pro 2020 series, Apple has recorded a landslide breakthrough in the world of Computer Tablet especially with the introduction of LiDAR Scanner. The device comes in two versions, the 11 and 12.9- inches screen with significant technological improvements. Now, that you have got a new iPad Pro 2020, don't struggle to get the best out of it. Here is a comprehensive guide to walk you through the nity-grity of using the device seamlessly from how you to set up the phone for the first time, configure the phone, get numerous tips and tricks to use your device, including troubleshooting seamlessly.

This instruction guide is also essential for iPhone switchers or novice Android phone users to easily navigate the iPad Pro models.

About the Author

Robert William is an Information Technology expert with over 15 years' experience in the ICT industry. He is an ardent follower of technological trends and personates in proffering solutions to complex problems. Robert holds a Bachelor's and a Master's Degree in Computer Science and Information Communication Technology, respectively, from MIT, Boston, Massachusetts.

Chapter One

Evolution of iPad Pro Series

An iPad is a tablet computer developed and first released in 2010 by Apple Inc. The tablet is used for seamless browsing on the web, reading and sending emails, reading e-books, playing games, playing videos, and much more. There have been a series of releases of iPad for a decade with different technological improvements. One of the significant releases is iPad Pro 12.9, which was released in November 2015 with a 12.9" display, 12MP Rear, and 7MP Front camera with 4GB RAM. It comes with a different internal capacity of 32/128/256GB. It has a capacity of 10,307mAh battery with Touch ID and Apple pencil introduced.

In March 2016, iPad Pro 9.7 was introducedvwith no significant improvement on the previous release. It comes with a 9.7" display, the same camera, internal storage, and Touch ID with iPad Pro 12.9 but with lesser RAM capacity (2GB) and battery capacity (7306mAh) compared to the previous version.

In June 2017, Apple released iPad Pro 12.9 with a bigger screen (12.9), bigger RAM (4GB), and higher battery capacity (10,891mAh). The internal storage comes in

64/256/512GB. Within the same month, iPad Pro 10.5 was released. It has the same features as iPad Pro 12.9 but with a smaller display of 10.5" and a lower battery capacity of 8134mAh.

In November 2018, another iPad Pro was launched with a 12.9" display, internal storage up to 1TB, 4GB RAM, and 9720mAh battery capacity. A face ID for biometric recognition was introduced. In the same month, iPad Pro 11 was released with a smaller display of 11" and a lower capacity battery of 7182mAh while other features are the same as iPad Pro 12.9 of 2018.

In March 2020, Apple released its latest iPad Pro version with significant improvements on the previous versions. These technological improvements on iPad Pro 2020 would be unfolded with time.

Chapter Two

iPad Pro 2020 Hardware

What's inside the box?

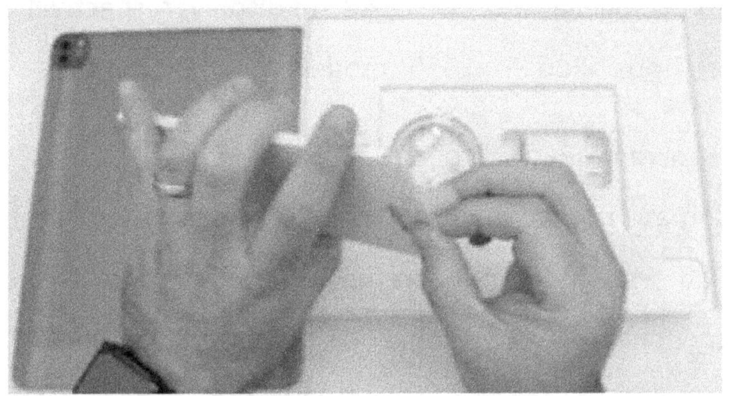

Contained in the box are;

- The phone (iPad Pro 2020).

- 18-wattUSB-C wall charger

- A USB-C power cable

- Instruction manual and terms & conditions

- An Apple sticker

iPad Pro 2020 Configuration

The iPad Pro 2020 comes In 11 and 12.9–inch size models, and it is available in silver and space grey colors. The 11-inch iPad Pro model is 9.74–inch (247.6mm) long and 7.02–inch (128.5mm) wide while the 12.9–inch model is 1.3–inch (33.0mm) longer and 1.44–inch

(86.4mm) wider. The 11-inch and 12-inch models have 2388 x 1668 display and 2732 x 2048 display, respectively. However, both iPad Pro 2020 models are 5.9mm thick.

Apple powers iPad Pro 2020 models with AA12Z processor, an upgraded version of A12X chips used in the 2018 iPad Pro and an 8-core CPU, an upgraded 8-core GPU for demanding tasks like 4k video editing and 3D models designing. The iPad Pro 2020 models come with 6GB RAM and 128GB – 1TB storage. It supports Wi-Fi 6, Bluetooth 5.0, 5G networks, and giga-class LTE for cellular. In both models, an Ultra wide-angle camera and a LiDAR scanner were introduced.

At the top of the iPad Pro, there is a sleep/wake button along with two speakers and two microphones. On the right side, there are volume up and down buttons, a magnetic connector to accessories, and a Nano-SIM tray on the cellular iPads model. There is a USB-C port between two speakers at the bottom while there is a microphone on the left side of the iPad Pro.

At the back, there is a camera bump containing a wide-angle camera, an Ultra wide-angle camera, a LiDAR Scanner, and a microphone.

The iPad Pro 11-inch model costs at $799 for 128GB of storage, $899 for 256GB, $1099 for 512GB and $1299 for 1TB. The iPad Pro 12.9-inch model costs at $999 for 128GB, $1099 for 256GB, $1299 for 512GB and $1499 for 1TB of storage. An additional $150 is applicable to acquire iPad Pro 2020 with cellular connectivity.

The Smart keyboard folio for the 11-inch and 12.9-inch models is available at about $179 and $199, respectively, while the Apple pencil 2 for both models is available at $129. The magic keyboard with a trackpad for 11-inch and 12.9-inch models is available at $299 and $349.

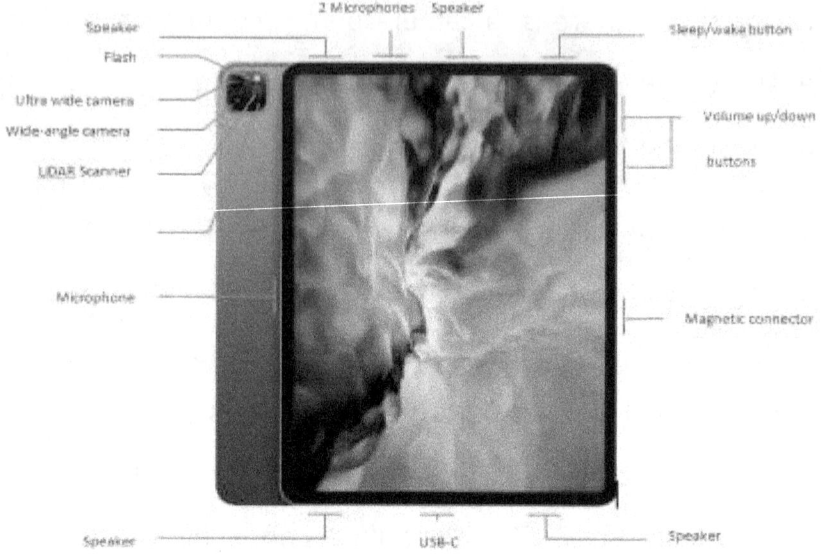

Cameras System

The iPad Pro 2020 camera system comes with two rear cameras, a front camera, and a LiDAR Scanner. The rear cameras are a 12-megapixel wide-angle camera with f/1.8 aperture and a 10-megapixel Ultra wide-angle camera with f/2.4 aperture with a large field of view.

The front camera is a True Depth 7-megapixel camera used for selfies and Face Time video. This camera supports Animoji and Memoji. One of the latest breakthroughs in the iPad Pro releases is LiDAR (Light Detection and Range) Scanner in the camera system of iPad Pro 2020 models. LiDAR Scanner enables you to measure objects up to five meters away from both indoors and outdoors.

Best Accessories for iPad Pro 2020 Models

Numerous accessories will help enhance functionality, increase productivity, and protect your iPad Pro. Among these accessories are:

* Magic keyboard

The Magic Keyboard is one of the breakthroughs of iPad in accessories over the years. Compared to the smart keyboard, it is a high-quality design product. It is designed with a trackpad for navigation and magnet all through the back cover to give a super solid attachment to the device. It has a smart connector to connect the keyboard to the iPad, and the keyboard has a backlight powered by the iPad. No battery, no pairing is needed to connect the keyboard to the iPad. The hinge design on the magic keyboard enables the iPad pro to adjust flexibly up to 130 degrees view angle.

Interestingly, the magic keyboard is also compatible with the iPad 2018 model. It also provides a second USB-C port for charging, leaving the one on your iPad Pro free for any other accessories. The magic keyboard is about $300 for 11" version and $350 for the 12.9" version.

- USB-C Apple Watch Charger

This is a traveling companion that enables you to charge your Apple Watch with your iPad pro. To charge your Apple Watch, plug the USB-C Apple Watch Charger to your iPad Pro and place the Apple Watch on it. You can also use the Apple Watch Charger with your Computer.

- Ravpower

This portable external battery can charge your device if you don't have access to plug your device to a wall. It has a USB-A and USB-C power delivery. It has a huge capacity of 15000mAh, and most importantly, it has a display where you can know the percentage of power left.

- Paper-like screen protector

This is a screen protector that makes you feel like writing or drawing on a piece of paper. It gives the iPad's screen more grips when using the Apple pencil, and it also reduces glare from the iPad's screen.

- iPad Smart Folio

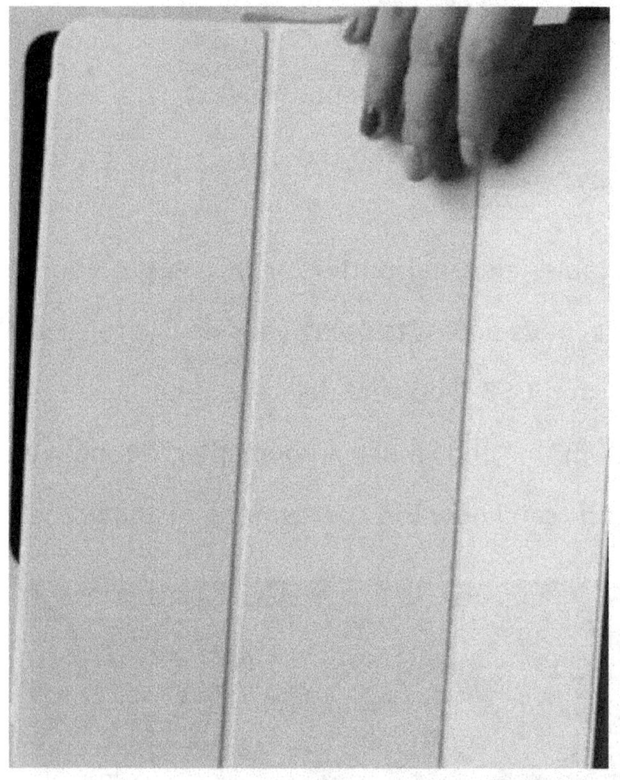

- Magic Mouse 2

The Magic Mouse 2 is rechargeable and works perfectly over Bluetooth. It is lightweight, portable, fits in hand so well, precise in its movement, and enables gestures to interact with your device. You can have up to 3 separate devices paired with it.

- Samsung SSD T5

Samsung portable Solid-State Drive T5 is one of the best external storage you can get. It provides seamless connectivity, portable, extremely fast in data transfer, and password protection to secure your data.

- Portable Console for Gaming

This is the Steel Series gaming console. It is connected to iPad   Pro 2020   via   Bluetooth for   seamless   gaming activities. It charges by a lightning cable via the lightning port on the controller.

- Apple Pencil 2

The new generation Apple pencil 2 was released alongside the 2018 iPad Pro. It looks slightly different from the Apple pencil 1 with the lightning connector and Cap went. It has one side flat, making it comfortable in hand. Also, there is an addition of a double-tap feature. To apply this, double-tap anywhere in the front end of the pencil, and the iPad will switch to from the eraser tool, making it incredibly quick and effective to fix your work mistakes. You can buy an Apple pencil from the Apple website or Amazon.

- Apple Pencil cases

This envelope Apple Pencil for protection

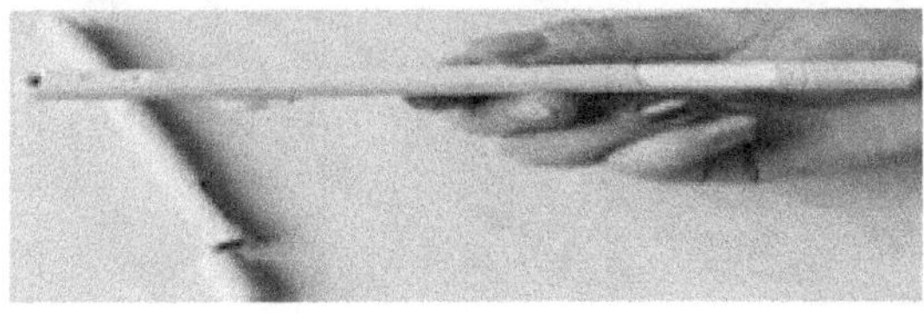

- Apple Pencil Stand

This is used to hold the Apple Pencil in a   position.

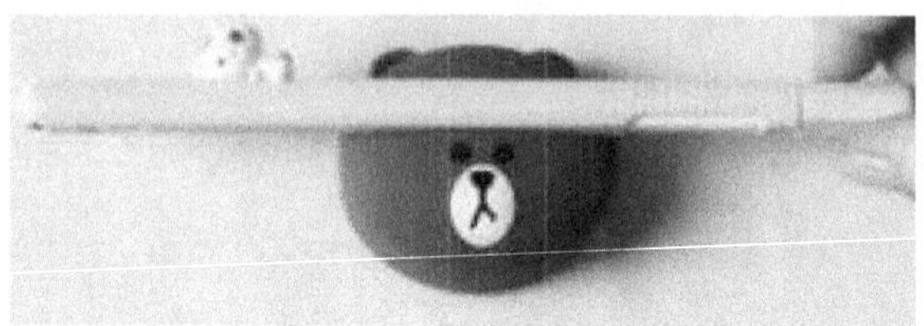

Paring Apple Pencil 2 with iPad Pro 2020

To pair the Apple Pencil with your iPad Pro 2020,

- Remove the cap on the pencil.

- Plug the pencil into the magnetic connector on the side of your device

- A dialog appears on the screen.

- Click on "Connect." The iPad is paired with your iPad until you restart the iPad.

Setting Apple Pencil 2 Double Tap

To set Apple pencil double-tap, go to settings and click on Apple Pencil in settings, then select from the available options which include: switch between current tool and eraser, switch between current tool and last tool used, show color palette, or disable altogether.

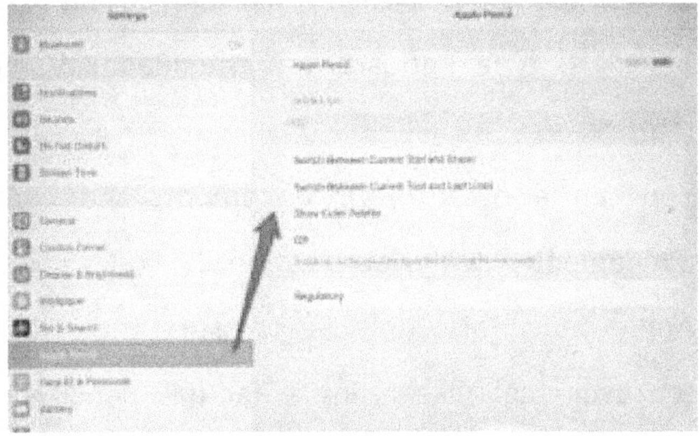

To adjust the double-tap duration, Click on settings

- Click non-General

- Tap on accessibility

- Tap on Apple Pencil

- Select from the available options, which include: Default, Slow,   and Slowest.

What can the Apple Pencil Do?

Some of the several functions of an Apple Pencil are outlined below.

- You can navigate almost anywhere on the iPad using an Apple pencil

- You can swipe down from the middle of the screen to bring spotlight like surge and use the pencil to type and activate the iPad key flipping feature.

- You can also sign your documents and contracts conveniently with Apple's pencil.

- Apple pencil also detects pressure and tilt, giving the user feels like using an actual pencil, pen, or marker.

Chapter Three

The Basics

Inserting the SIM Card

If you have purchased iPad Pro 2020 cellular model, follow the steps below to insert a Nano-SIM card.

- Insert the ejection pin into the hole on the tray to loosen the tray.

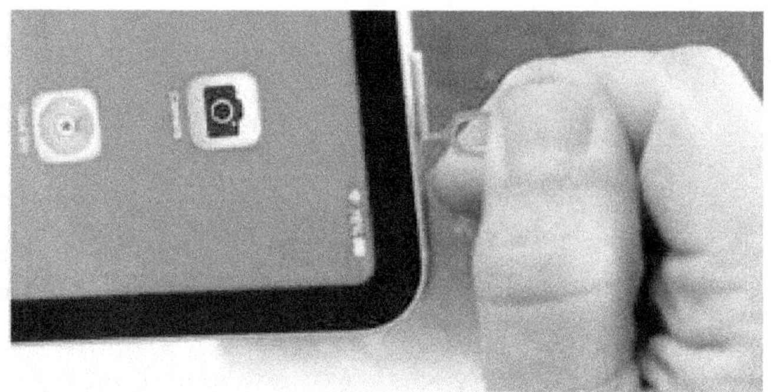

- Place the SIM card on the SIM card slot with the gold-colored contacts facing downwards and ensure that it lay flat and keyed in.

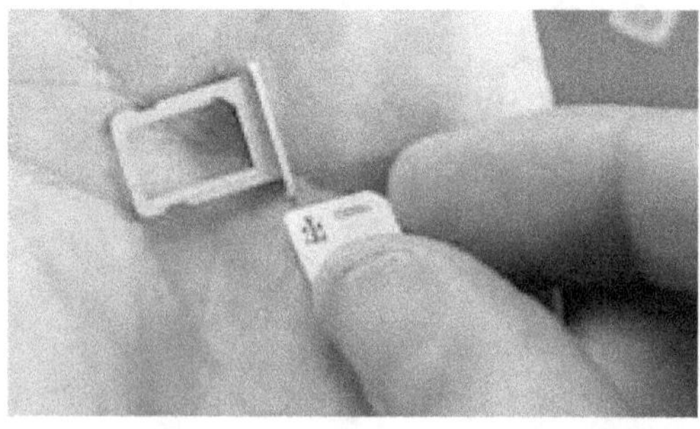

- Now, carefully insert the SIM tray back to the slot.

Initial Setup

Before you can use your newly procured iPad Pro 2020 model, you are required to initiate some setup. You can set up your new iPad pro or restore information backed up on your iCloud account from your old iPad or iPhone. To go about this initial setup and transfer data from your old phone to your iPad Pro, follow the steps below.

- Press and hold the power button until the Apple logo appears on the screen. This may take a few seconds.

- Swipe up the screen to reveal the language options then, select the language of your choice.

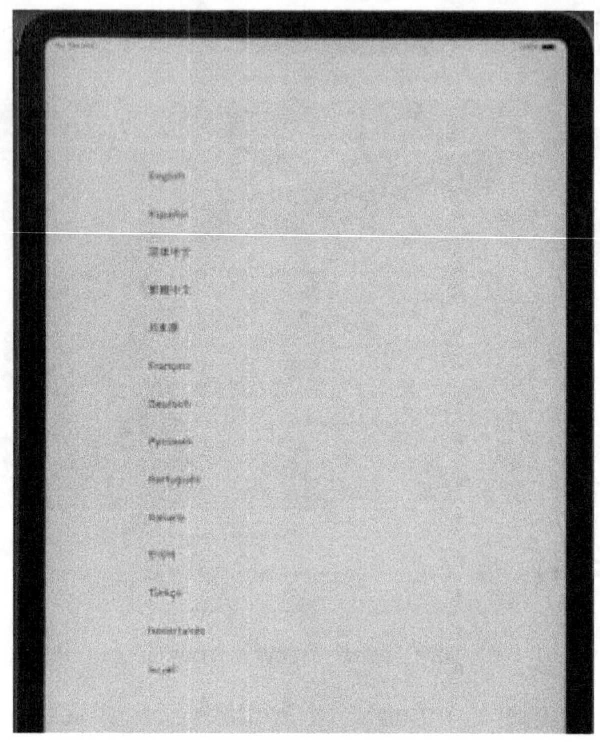

- Then, swipe up to select your country or region from the list of countries and regions.

- If you have an old iPhone or iPad running iOS 11 or later, bring it near the iPad to sign in and set up your new iPad automatically by selecting the "Quickstart" option, else you select the "set up manually" option at the bottom to set up your device manually.

- Tap on "set up manually" option

- You are prompted to choose a Wi-Fi Network. Choose your Network and enter your password.

- You are then prompted to Apple Data & Privacy. Click on "continue."

- Next is the Face ID setting for authentication. Skip this for now and tap on "set up later in settings."

- You are then prompted to create a passcode that is used to protect your data and also used to unlock your iPad. Enter your six-character passcode. Renter the passcode again for confirmation.

- Next is "Apps & Data." Apps and Data window enables you to select how you want to transfer Apps and Data into your new iPad Pro. You can restore your desired Apps & Data from iCloud backup, Mac or PC, or Android device. You also have the option not to transfer any App or Data from any device if you so desire by selecting "Don't Transfer Apps & Data." For now, tap on "Don't Transfer Apps & Data."

- Next is "Apple ID." Your Apple ID is the account through which you access all Apple services. Enter your Apple ID in the space provided.

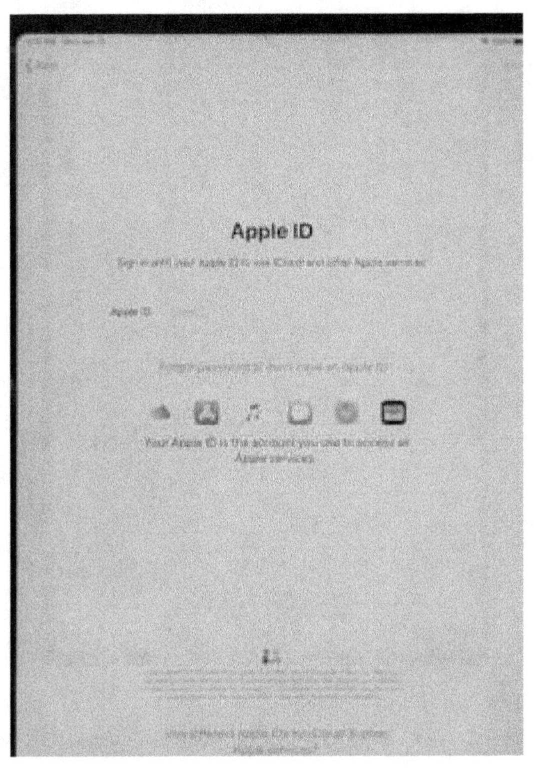

- Next in the set up process is a window requesting you to keep your iPad up to date. Keeping your iPad up to date enables you to get the latest Apple features, security, and improvements by updating ios automatically. So click on "continue" to enable updates automatically.

- Next, you will be prompted to set up the Apple Pay, as shown above. When you set up the Apple pay, it enables you to add a debit or credit card to your Apple wallet. This enables you to make seamless purchases on the Apple stores and any other platform that accepts Apple pay. You may choose to skip this during set up and configure it later in the wallet App. For now, click on "set up later in settings" to continue with the iPad set up process.

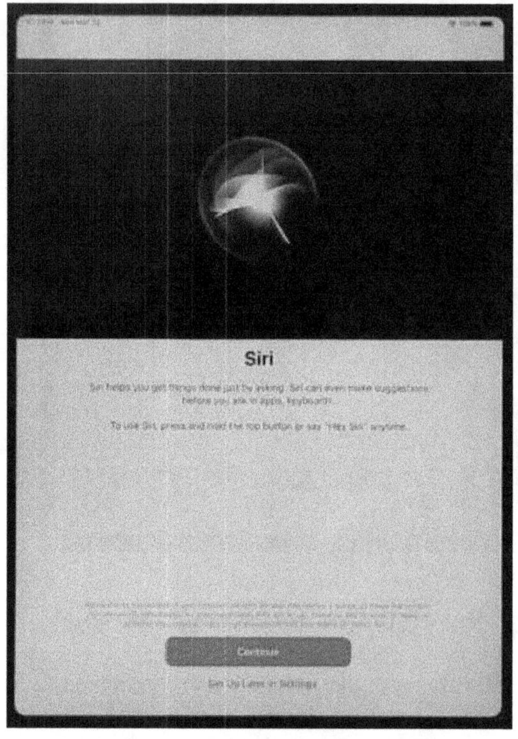

- Next is "Siri" as shown above. Siri helps you get things done by asking. You may also choose to skip this during set up and configure it later in settings. For now, click on "set up later in settings" to continue with the iPad set up process.

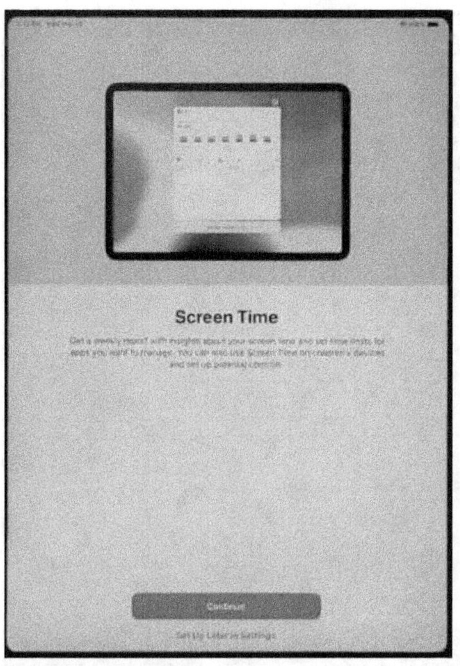

- Next is "Screen Time." Screen Time enables you to limit the usage of your iPad or App(s) on it. Skip this for now and tap on "Set up Later in settings" to move to the next level.

- Next is "App Analytics." App Analytics enables you to share data with developers about your iPad performance. To protect your privacy, tap on "Don't Share" and move on to the next stage.

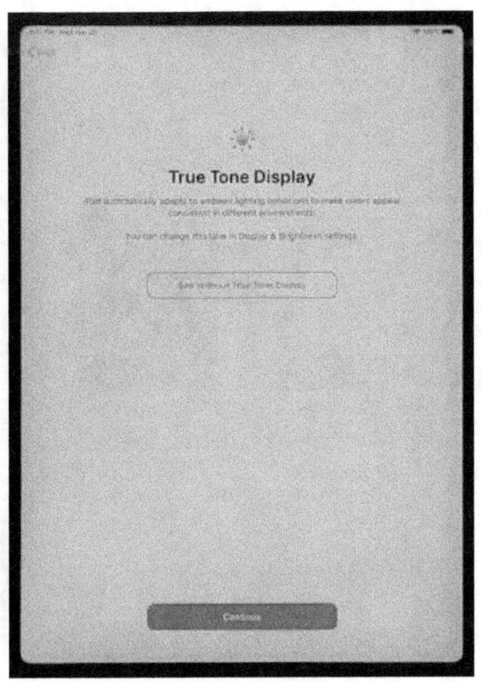

- Next is "True Tone Display." True Tone Display enables the iPad to automatically adjust to ambient lighting conditions, making colors appear consistent in different situations. Tap on continue.

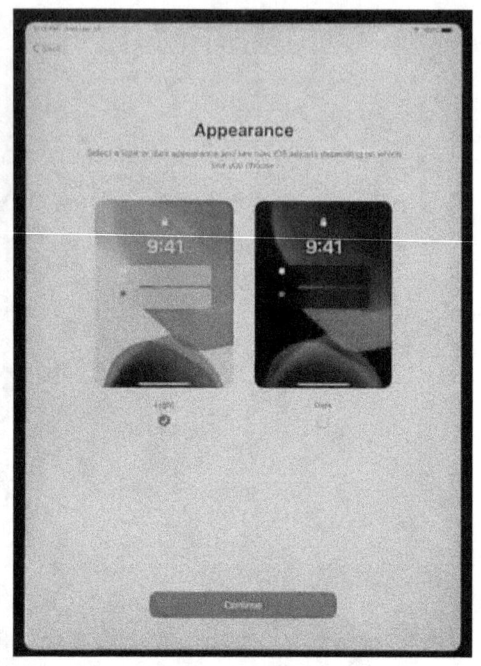

- Next is "Appearance." Appearance enables you to choose between dark mode and light mode appearances for your iPad screen. Select your preferred mode and tap "continue" to move to the next stage.

- Next is "Quick Access to the Dock." This is a pointer to inform you that you will swipe up from the bottom edge to show the Dock and then release. Just click on "Continue" to move to the next stage.

- Next is "Switch Between Recent Apps." This is a pointer to inform you how to switch Between Recent Apps. Just click on "Continue" to move to the next stage.

- You are prompted to a "Welcome to iPad" window, which signifies the end of the initial set up of your new iPad Pro 2020. Other customizations will be done through settings with time.

You can transfer data from your old iPad to the new one through iTunes, iCloud or Syncios transfer. Syncios iPad Transfer is a software purposely made to enable iPad data transfer, and it's preferable due to no data loss.

To transfer data through Syncios transfer, follow the steps below.

- Download and install syncios iPad transfer software on your computer
- plug your old iPad to the computer with a USB cable and initiate syncios iPad transfer
- Select the file type
- Press "Shift" and select the files listed on the panel
- Then, click "Export" and choose the backup location in your computer. Then, disconnect your old iPad
- Click "OK" after the backup completed.
- Plug your new iPad and click "Import."
- Press "Shift" and select all the files you intend to transfer to your new iPad
- Then, click "Open."

Chapter Four

Swipes Gesture Controls

IPad Pro 2020 uses gestures to navigate, multitask, access various features and apps. The device is enriched with new gesture controls that enable seamless navigation.

Waking the device

To wake up the iPad pro-2020, a single tap on the screen. This is a simple way to check the read notification, time, or adjust media playback.

Switching Apps & Going Home

IPad has always had two unique gestures: the five fingers to close the apps and four fingers to swipe between apps. With your five fingers, make a pinching motion spread across the open app to close it while a swipe to switch between apps with your four fingers. To go back to the home screen at any time, swipe up from the bottom of the screen quickly, and the home screen appears.

Accessing the Dock

To view the app dock, swipe up from the bottom of the display about an inch. The app-doc will appear to enable you to switch between apps or drags app icons to either side of the screen to split your screen. Then, you swipe down from the app doc to hide it.

Adding an App to the Dock

To move an app to the dock, follow the steps below.

- Navigate to the Home screen containing the App icon

- Tap and hold on the App icon and then drag it to the dock at the bottom of the screen

- Then, release your finger to drop the App in the dock.

Removing an App from the dock

- Swipe upward from the bottom edge of the screen to reveal the dock.
- Tap and hold on the App icon in the dock and drag it to the Home Screen.
- Then, release your finger to drop the App in the Home Screen.

Multitasking in iPad Pro 2020

Multitasking helps to increase the productivity of your iPad as you access the apps effortlessly and navigate seamlessly.

Multitasking involves: Slide Over, Split Over, and Picture-in-picture.

Open Apps in Slide Over

When you open an app in slide over, you will view an app within another app. It enables you to use two apps simultaneously with your primary app display on the full screen behind the second one. To slide over, follow the steps below.

- Open an app on your iPad Pro

- Swipe from the bottom of the screen to access the dock

- Tap and hold the App you intend to open from the dock

- Drag the App into the middle of the screen and release it.

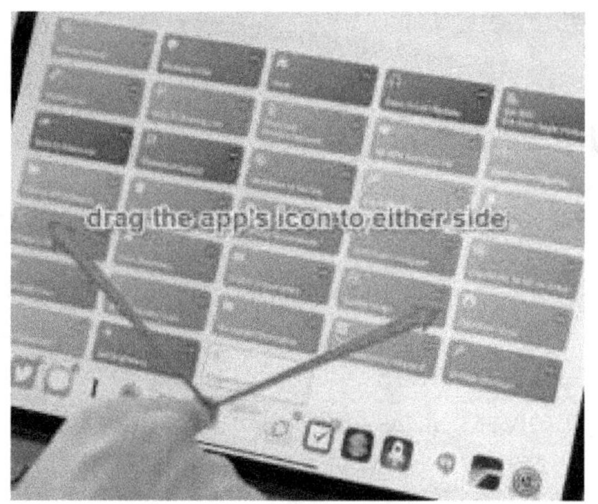

To close the slide cover at the right side of the screen, swipe it to the right side to close it and swipe to the left to bring it back.

Open Apps in Split View

Split view mode enables you to access two different apps simultaneously. You can have an app open on one side of the screen, and another one opens on the other side of the screen. You can even open two windows from the same app to simultaneously view a different portion of the app. To split view, follow the steps below.

- Open an app

- Swipe up from the bottom of the screen to access the Dock

- Tap and hold on the second app you intend to open from the Dock

- Drag the app from the Dock to the left or right side of the screen and release

- Resize your app window by dragging the app divider to the center of the screen

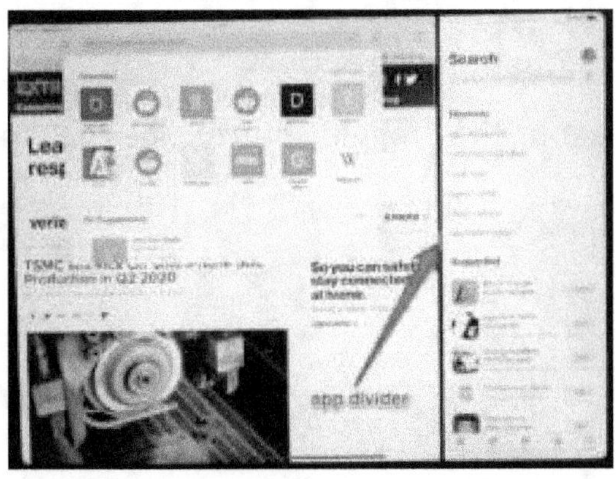

To close split view, drag the app divider over the app you want to close.

How to Enable and Use Picture in Picture

Picture in Picture is a feature that enables you to multitask on your iPad. It allows videos you're playing and Face Time video calls to continue when you swipe up to go home and use other apps. This feature works on any website that plays videos, but if you want it to work on YouTube, you have to the mobile version of YouTube, which is "m.youtube.com." Before you use Picture in Picture, ensure you enable it. To enable this feature,

- Go to "Settings"
- Scroll down and tap on "General."
- Tap on "Multitasking & Dock."
- Switch on the toggle button beside Picture in Picture

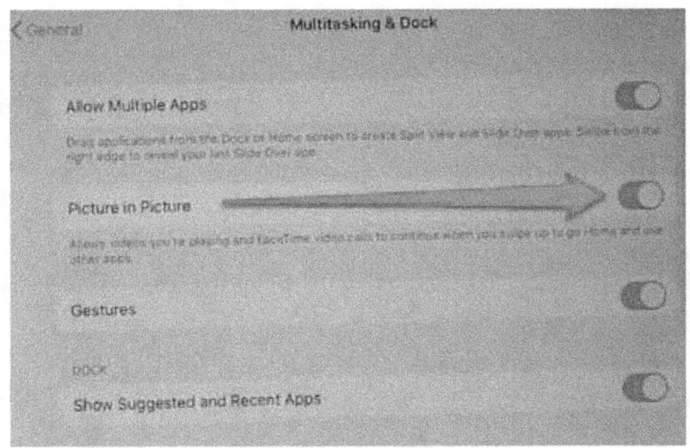

To use Picture in Picture,

- ✓ Play your video
- ✓ Tap on Picture in Picture icon at the top-right corner of your screen as shown below.

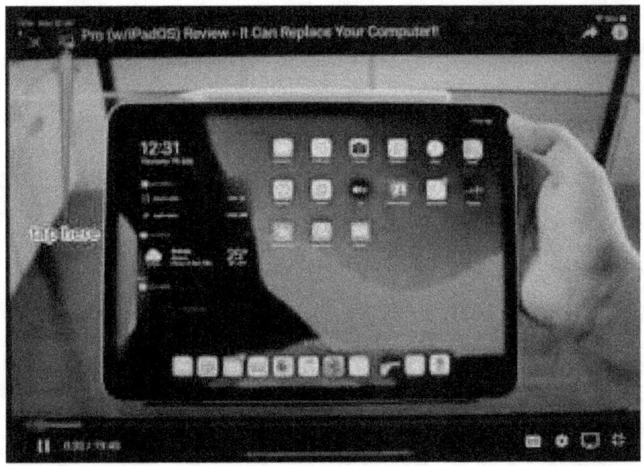

✓ Then, go back to your Home screen. You will see the video floating. You can minimize it, place it wherever you like on the screen.

Force Close an App

To force close an app, open app switcher, and swipe up on the app.

View Recent Files in the App

To access the files you worked on in an App, press and hold the App icon.

Accessing the Control Center

The Control center is where you can adjust settings and other handy features of the iPad. To access the control center, swipe down from the top-right corner of the screen.

Accessing Notification center

The notification center is where you view your recent notifications. To access the notification center, swipe down from the top middle of the display.

How to turn ON, OFF & RESTART your iPad

To turn OFF your device, press and hold on the sleep/wake button and volume down simultaneously. Then, slide to power off.

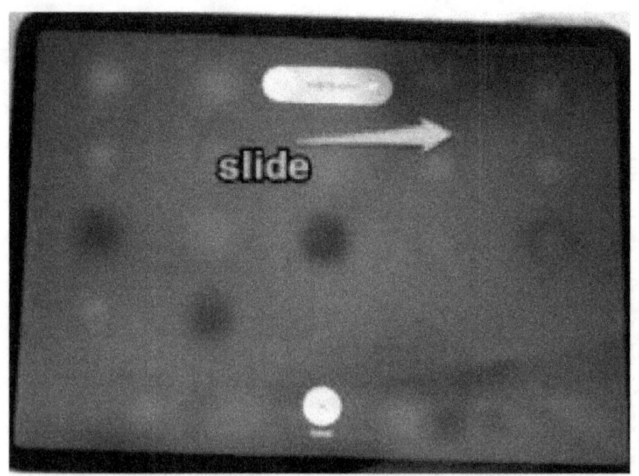

To restart the iPad, follow the steps below.

- ✓ Press the volume up
- ✓ Press the volume down   in a quick succession
- ✓ Then, press and hold the sleep/wake button until the screen goes black. Soon after, you will see the Apple logo appears.

To turn ON the iPad Pro, press and hold on the sleep/wake button until the apple logo appears.

Copy, Paste, Do and Redo

To copy a selected text, pinch in with your 3 fingers and pinch out with your 3 fingers to paste the text.

To undo, swipes to the left with your 3 fingers and swipes to the right to redo.

Chapter Five

iPad Pro 2020 Models Applications

JustWatch

This is an Application used to find one's favorite movies or TV shows to watch. It is a streaming guide for movies and TV shows, enabling you to know new releases of these items.

MyRadar

MyRadar is an App used to check the weather conditions of different places around the world. It is a great App to view weather information as posted by weather channels around the globe.

Retouch

This App is used to remove unwanted objects from images, especially when you do many photos taken and want to do quick editing. When you finished the download, and you launched the App, the video takes the picture right there from your camera, or you get access to your camera.

- Select the image
- Tap on "remove objects"

- Select the items to be removed and tap on "Go."

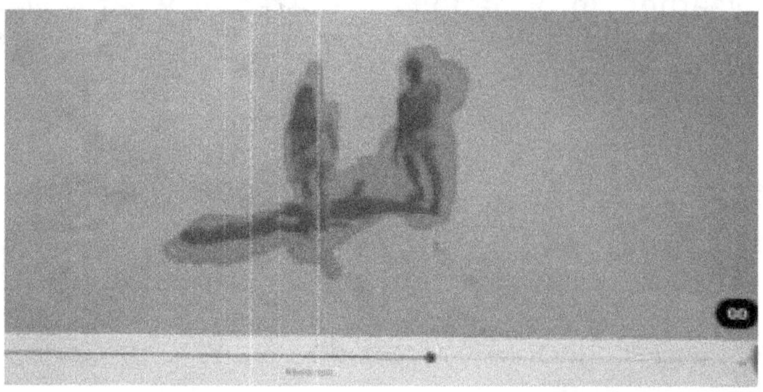

Vellum Wallpapers

This is a great app available on the App Store with many free pictures from which you can select and download to change   your iPad's look.

QuickNote

QuickNote is an Application that you can use to create a notebook and take your note.

Pocket

Pocket is an App used to save articles, videos,   and stories you   intend to view later.

Kitchen Stories

Kitchen Stories is a community-driven App where you get free recipes, videos, and articles about cooking and baking. You can also publish your recipes to the world through this App.

Call of Duty M

This is a gaming App that supports four console controllers.

Calendar

This is an App that enables you to learn new languages on your iPad.

Udemy

Udemy is a platform where you can upload your question(s) and get an answer(s). You can create a question

Duolingo

Duolingo is an App through which you can learn new languages on your iPad.

Notability

Notability is an App for note-taking. It enables you to take note, erase, cut, and move parts of a text by using the App's available tools.

Measure App

The measure is an App meant to carry out measurements around the house and office. With the measure App, you can measure the length, height, and width of objects.

To use the measure App, follow the steps below.

- Launch the App from your Home screen

- Position the white dot to your start point

- Tap on the "+" button to select the start point

- Move thew hite dot to your endpoint

- Tap on the "+" button to select the endpoint

- Take the final measurement that appears in the middle of the line joining the start point and the endpoint.

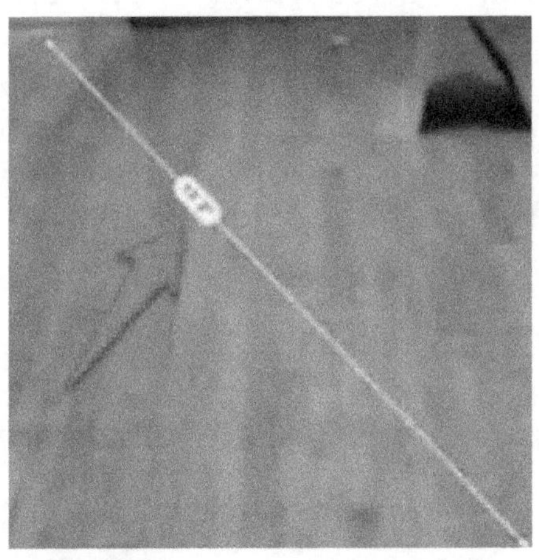

How to Download Apps from the App Store

App Store is a platform developed by Apple, where you can download free and paid mobile Apps. To download the app,

- Tap on the App store on your Home Screen

- Please search for the app you intend to download and click on it
- Tap on "Get" if it is a free app or tap on the price of the app

How to Rearrange the Apps in iPad

To organize Apps on the iPad, press and hold the App icon in the Home Screen until they start wiggling with "x" on them. Then, press and drag the Apps to your desired location one after the order. You can also rearrange the Apps in the dock.

Inserting Apps in a Folder

You can arrange apps inside a folder to prevent the Home screen from being clumsy. To insert the app in a folder,

- Activate the wiggle mode
- Click and drag the app onto another app to automatically create a folder and add the apps into the folder
- Rename the folder if you wish

To remove any app from a folder, click on the app and drag it out.

Chapter Six

Settings

How to enable Battery percentage

When you enable battery percentage on your iPad, you will be able to know the current level of your battery at a glance, which is shown at the top-right corner of your screen. To enable the battery percentage,

- Go to settings and tap on "Battery."
- Enable the toggle button beside the battery percentage

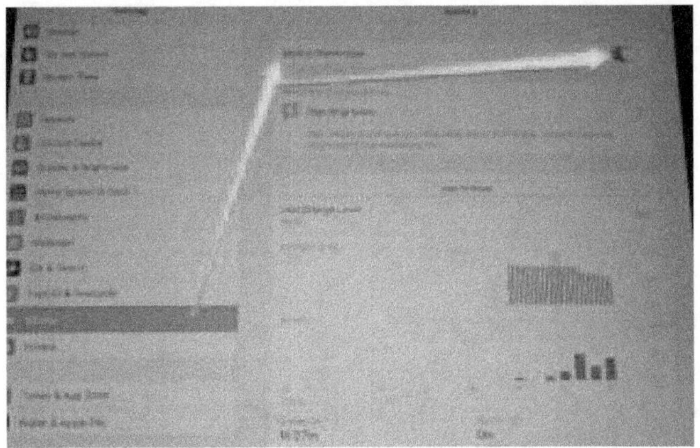

How to Customize Control Center

To customize the control center,

- go to "Settings."
- Scroll down and tap on the "Control Centre."
- Tap on "Customize Controls"

- To add a control, tap on the "+" sign beside the control under "More Controls."

- To remove a control, tap on the "-"sign beside the control under "Include."

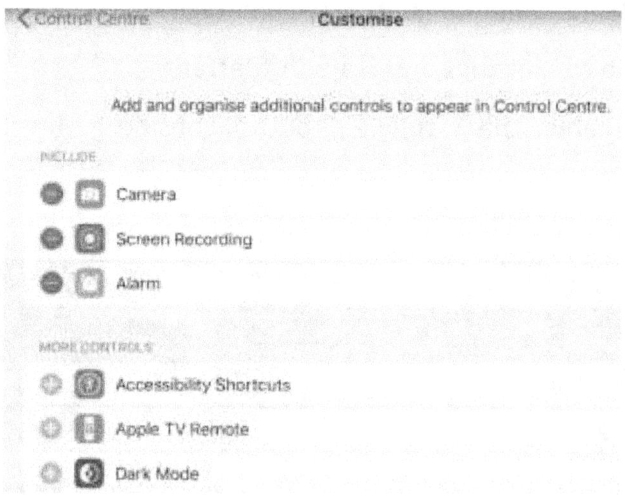

How to take Screenshot

To screenshot on your iPad Pro, press on the power button and the volume up simultaneously and quickly release them. The screenshot appears at the lower-left corner of the device. You can tap on the screenshot to add drawings and text, swipe left to discard it, or search for it in your photos later.

Alternatively, you can screenshot by using the apple pencil to swipe diagonally from the screen's corner.

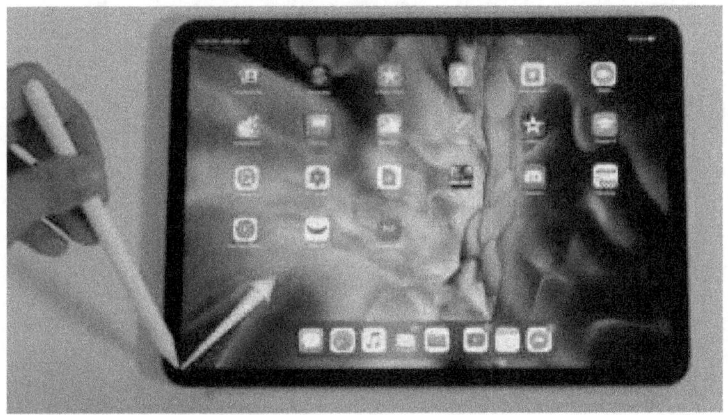

Enable/Disable Dark Mode

Dark mode allows you to change the screen look of your phone. The dark mode is suitable for your eye, and it makes your battery last longer, and it's even cool. The dark mode is meant to give Apple's pre-installed apps on iPad a dark background and a little aesthetics. When you activate dark mode, your device battery life is preserved. To activate dark mode,

- Go to settings

- Scroll down and tap on "Display & Brightness."

- You are prompted to select either light or dark.

- Click on the "dark" button.

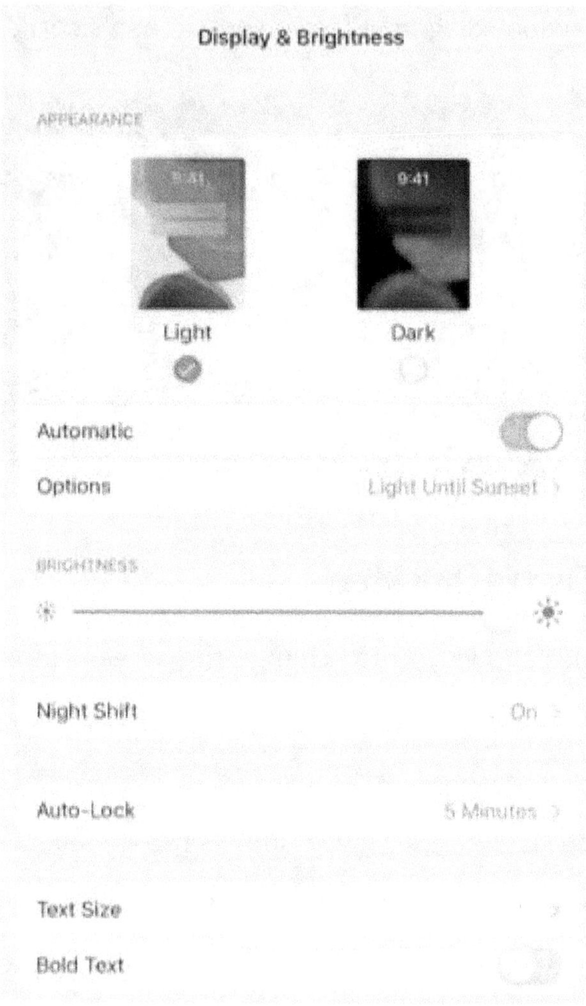

- Then, click on the "Automatic" toggle button to enable the dark mode to turn ON whenever dark.

- When you click on option other than automatic, you will have a sunset to sunrise or create a custom schedule for light appearance and dark appearance

- Select "Dark" to activate dark mode.

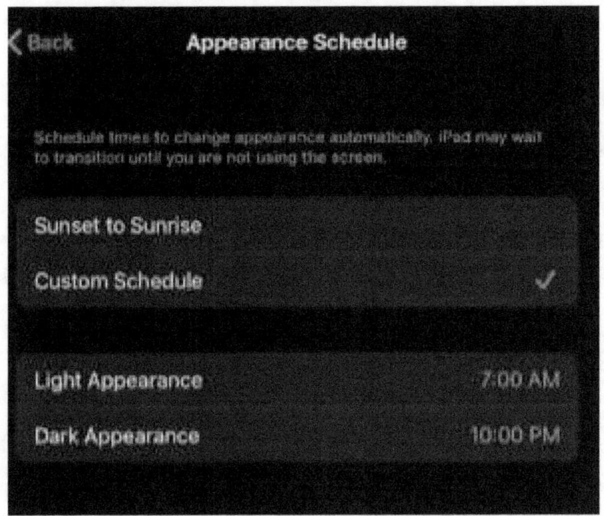

Alternatively, you can enable dark mode through the control center.

- Swipe down from the top - right corner of the screen to access the control center
- Tap and hold on right in the middle of the screen brightness setting icon
- Click on the dark mode button

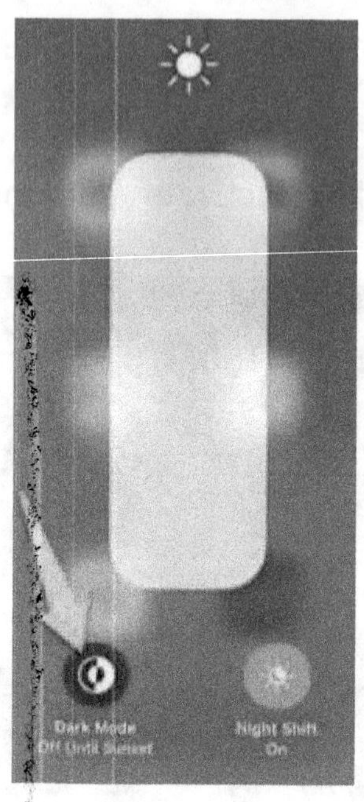

To add dark mode to the control center so that you don't have to go through so many steps,

- Click on "Settings"

- Scroll down and tap on the "Control Center."

- You will be prompted with control center settings.

- Click on "Custom controls."

- Under the "more controls," click on the plus sign beside "Dark Mode."

- Then, Dark Mode appears under the "include."

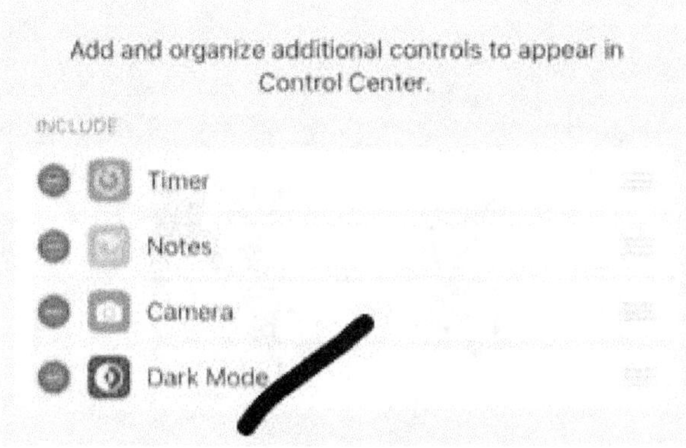

How to activate Automatic Dark Mode

You may want to customize "Dark Mode" such that it comes up automatically at night, and "Light Mode" comes up automatically at day time. To achieve this,

- Go to "Settings."

- Scroll down and tap on "Display & Brightness."

- Click on the toggle button for automatic to turn it ON

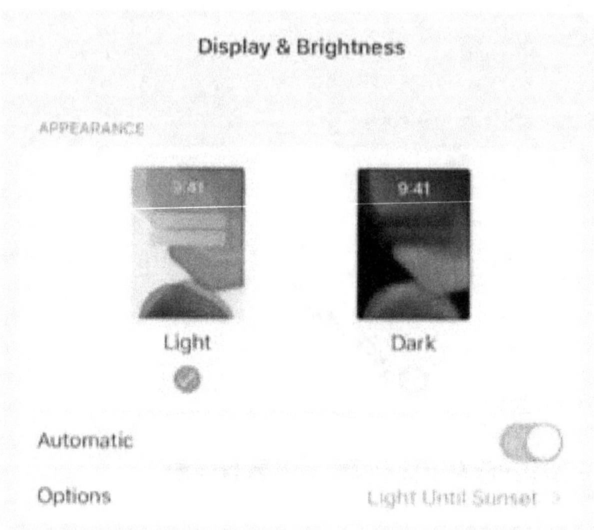

How to change wallpaper

To change the wallpaper on iPad pro-2020,

- Go to settings

- Click on a wallpaper and select any wallpaper of your choice.

- Then, click on "set." You will be prompted with three options: Set lock screen set Home Screen and set both.

- Click on "Set Lock Screen" if you intend to set the selected wallpaper as a lock screen.

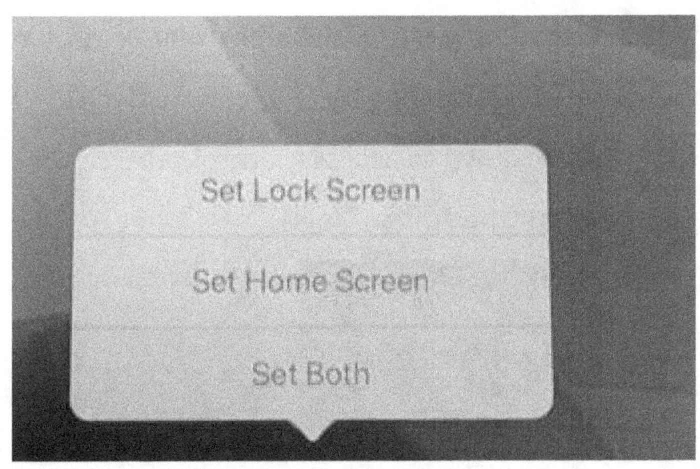

How to enable Tap to Wake

Since the iPad has no home button, you can tap to wake the device. To enable this tap to wake functionality,

- go to "settings."

- scroll down and click on "general."

- Then, click on "accessibility" and tap on the "tap to wake" toggle button.

Activating instant Do Not Disturb Mode

The "Do not disturb Mode" deactivates both visual and sound notification from calls, text messages, e-mails, and other alerts. This is very useful when you don't want any distractions, especially while driving or in a meeting. To activate this functionality,

- Swipe down to access control center
- Tap on the "moon" logo.

Setting Screen Time

Screen Time enables the iPad user to control the time spent on the apps or the device in general. It is a useful tool that allows you to put some checks on how the iPad is used.

Through screen time, you can get a weekly activity summary of how the iPad is used. You will see which AppApp is mostly used, how many times the iPad is picked up, etc. You can set a daily time limit for each AppApp and the iPad entirely. A section called "always allow" that when enabled for some apps, those apps will always be available even when the screen time elapsed. To set downtime in screen time, follow the steps below.

- go to "Settings."
- Scroll down and tap on Screen Time
- Tap on "Down Time" and tap on the toggle switch beside it to switch it ON.
- choose the start time and end time for the Down Time

How to bypass Downtime Limit

If you try to access an App when it is not available, you will receive a time limit warning. To gain access to such an App, follow the steps below.

- Tap on "Ignore Limit."
- Tap on "Permit Me in 5 minutes" to snooze. This will enable you to access the App before the downtime is activated.
- Tap on "Ignore Limit For Today" to unlock completely
- Tap on "Cancel" to accept the limit and move on.

Setting up Face ID on iPad Pro 2020

If you skipped setting Face ID during the initial set up of your iPad Pro, here are the steps to set up the Face ID.

- Go to "settings."
- Scroll down and tap on "Face ID & passcode."
- Enter your passcode
- Tap on "Set up Face ID" and click on "Get started."
- Position your face within the camera frame
- Scan your face by moving your head slowly to complete the circle
- Click "Continue" to scan your face for a second time.
- Then, click on "Done."
- Setting Two-Face ID's

You may want to set up two-Face ID to enable two-person to unlock the iPad Pro 2020. To set two-Face ID,

- go to "settings."
- Scroll down and tap on "Face ID & passcode
- Enter your passcode
- Tap on "Set an alternate Appearance."

How to reset Face ID

If your iPad was unable to recognize your face for some reason, like your face swell up, you could reset your face ID at any time.

- go to "Settings."
- Scroll down and tap on "Face ID."
- Enter your passcode and tap on "Reset Face ID."

Navigating your iPad Pro with TrackPad

A cursor will appear in your display when you interact with the trackpad and disappear when you stop using it. Some of the navigations are listed below.

- When you move the cursor over an app, the App will be highlighted to show it's selected.
- To bring out the app switcher, swipe up the trackpad with three fingers and hold
- To slide over, move the cursor over to the screen's right side until slide over the window appears.
- To close the slide over, move the cursor to the right side until the slide is closed.

- To return to the Home screen, click the bar at the bottom of the screen or swipe up with three fingers.

- To right-click or perform a secondary click, click on the trackpad with two fingers.

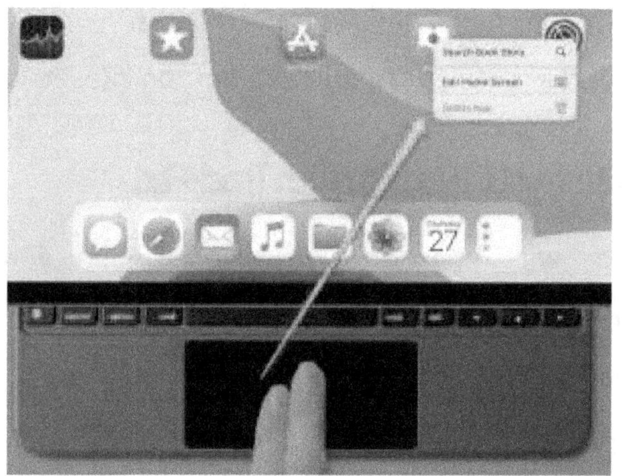

- To Zoom, pinch in and out

- To bring up the Dock, move the cursor to the bottom of the screen until the Dock appears

Customizing Cursor Settings

To customize the cursor settings,

- go to "Settings."

- Scroll down and tap on "General."

- Click on "Trackpad."

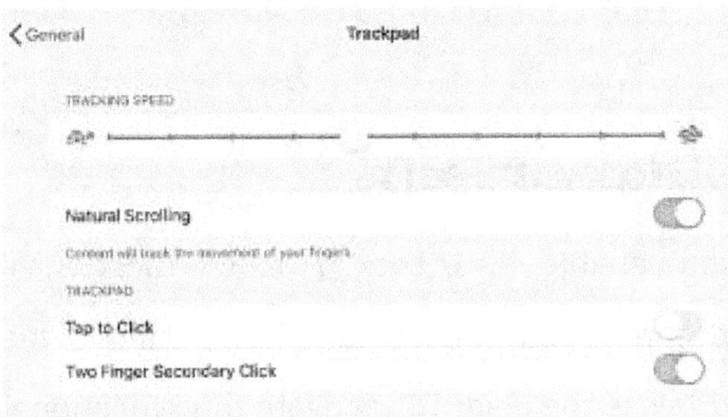

Use the slider to adjust cursor tracking speed. You can also turn ON/OFF "Natural scrolling, Tap to click, and Two Fingers secondary click."

To customize your cursor settings even more,

- Click on accessibility on the "Settings" sidebar

- Click on "Pointer control."

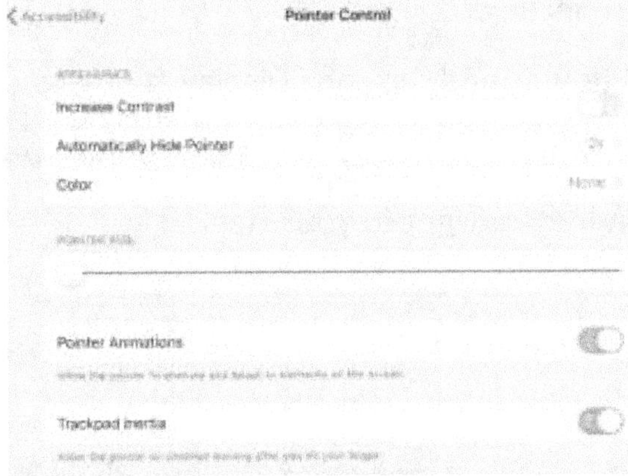

Here, you can automatically hide the pointer, select the pointer's color, and change the pointer size hide pointer.

Lock and Unlock your iPad Pro

When you enable this Lock /Unlock functionality on your iPad, the Ipad automatically lock /unlock when you open and close the iPad. To activate this functionality, go to "Settings."

scroll down and tap on "Display & Brightness."
Then, enable the lock/unlock toggle button.

How to Adjust Brightness

To adjust the brightness of the iPad Pro, follow the steps below.

- go to "Settings."
- scroll down and tap on "Display & Brightness."
- Adjust the brightness by moving the brightness button left or right to your taste

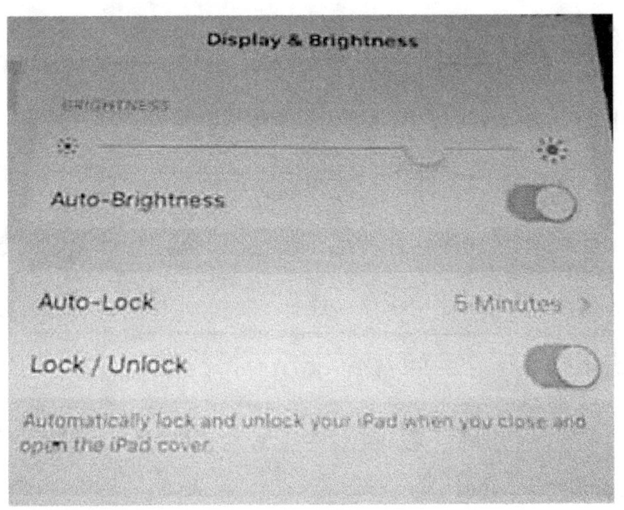

How to Adjust Media Volume

Volume determines the sound's loudness when you are listening to music, playing video, or games on your phone. You can control the volume of your iPad Pro; use the volume up/volume down.

Alternatively, you can adjust the volume by

- go to settings,
- scroll down and tap on "General."
- tap on "Sounds." Then, tap and drag the volume slider left to reduce the volume and drag to the right to increase the volume.

Turn off auto screen rotation.

When this feature is enabled, the screen of your phone rotates automatically when the phone orientation changes. To turn off auto screen rotation, follow the steps below.

- Swipe down from the top-right corner of the display to access the control center
- Click on the "auto rotate" icon to lock/unlock the screen rotation.

How to enable Tap to Wake

When tap to wake is enabled, you have to tap on the iPad screen to make it comes live from sleep. To enable this functionality,

- go to "Settings."

- Scroll down and tap on "General."

- Tap on "Accessibility" and then enable "tap to wake" by putting ON the toggle button beside it

How to create your Animoji

With the new camera features, you can create your own Animoji. To do this,

- go to messages

- Select the picture you want

- Click on "+" besides the pictures to create your Animoji

- Click on "Get Started."

- You are provided with different picture options and colors that you can select to create your Animoji

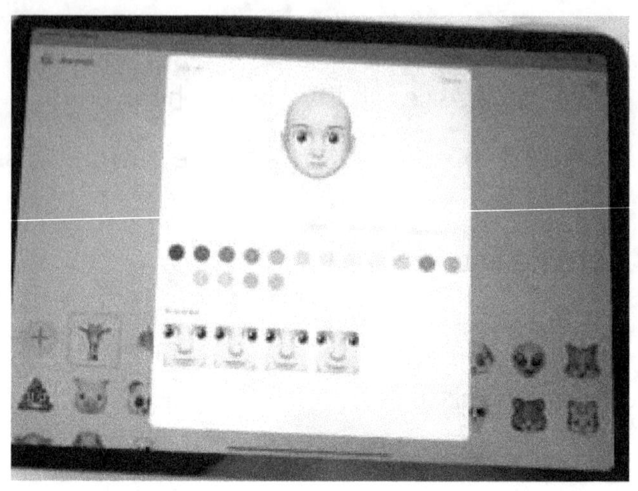

Enable Shortcut to Notes

When you enable shortcuts to Notes on your iPad, a tap with Apple pencil on the screen will automatically take you to Apple Note. To enable this feature,

- go to "Settings."

- Scroll down and tap on "Note."

- Tap on "Access Note from Lock Screen." You will be   prompted with   four options: OFF(preset option), Always create New Note, Resume last Note created on Lock Screen, and Resume Last Note Viewed on Notes App.

Locking your Note

You may want to protect your notes from unauthorized access to the contents. To do this, follow the steps below:

- Open the Note app on your iPad
- Open an existing note or create a new note.
- Tap on the share button at the top right corner of the display
- Enter your password
- Tap on "Done."

How to activate Home Button

iPad Pro 2020 models were released without Home Button. Users have to swipe up from the button of the screen to return to the Home screen. If you are used to having this wonderful functionality, the good news is that you can activate a virtual Home Button and makes it behaves like a real Home Button. To do this, follow the steps below:

- go to "Settings" from the Home screen
- scroll down and tap on "General."
- Tap on "Accessibility."

- Scroll down to the interaction section and tap on "Assistive Touch."

- Enable the toggle button. A floating button appears on the screen.

To make it work as a real Home Button,

- go to settings

- tap on "General."

- tap on "Accessibility." Under "Customize the top-level menu," add "Home."

Customizing Video Quality

When it comes to your recording, your camera has several ways to record several qualities. To customize them,

- go to "Settings."

- scroll down and tap on "Camera."

- Tap on "record video." Select from the options provided

How to enable Notification

Notifications are reminders that show on the screen to alerts you whenever your attention is required in any app. When you are sent a text message, for example, and a badge appears on the screen, it is a notification to tell you there is a message. Setting notification enables you to see only the ones you like to see and determine how they appear on your device's screen.

To enable notification,

- go to " Settings" on your Home screen
- tap on "Notification" and select the app you want to receive notification
- Then, enable "Allow notification."

Deactivating annoying pop ups

Depending on the sites you have visited, you may be getting some pesky pop-ups like you have won some gift items. These malware slips in like a virus when you visit a questionable and unsecured site or download some apps without thorough verification. If this is not taken care of in time, it might damage your device or reveal vital information from your device. To prevent this from escalating, close the pop-ups promptly as they appear and don't click on the close "x" button that appears on the ad. It will only end up taken you another ad. To avoid being taken to another ad, close your browser by swiping it up. You can then clear your browsing history.

To clear browsing history,

- go to "Settings."
- Scroll down and tap on "Safari."
- Then, clear the browsing.

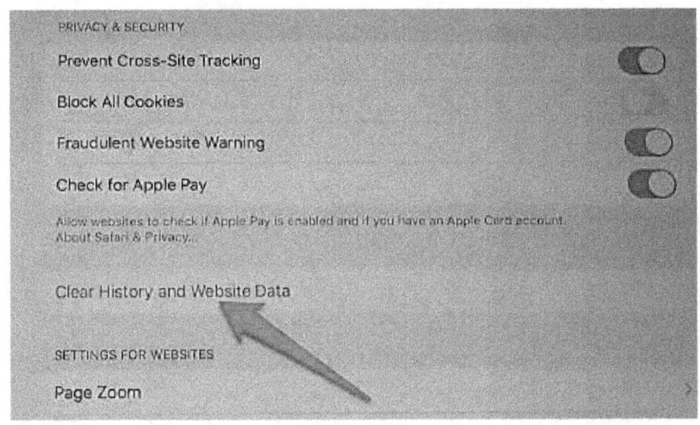

You can carry out a complete factory reset if "clear History" doesn't work for you. Meanwhile, before you embark on a factory reset, you ensure your information is backed up to the cloud. You may also install a Safari pop up blocker on your device and don't forget to enable "Fraudulent website warning safari" on your iPad. In all, desist from visiting unsecured websites.

Apple Pay

Apple Pay is a mobile payment platform designed to free users from using cards and cash. The system uses Near Field Communication (NFC) and Magnetic Secure Transmission to make payment when you tap your iPhone or iPad on a payment terminal. Apple pay cash enables users to send money through iMessage or Split-the-bill, and payment has to be confirmed with Face ID.

How to Add Card to Apple Pay

The mobile payment system uses tokenization technology to ensure your card is secured. Once your card is added to the App, a virtual account number is generated, not disclosed to any other person. Your phone may be stolen. Apple Pay allows you to delete your account details remotely to avoid unauthorized access. To add a card to your Apple pay wallet, follow the steps below.

- Open wallet app
- Tap on the "+" icon and scan your card
- Then, follow bank guidelines
- Click "Done"

Your card is now added to the Wallet App and ready for use on Apple pay.

How to Remove Used Pass

Wallet App is a way to integrate Apple pay into your iPad. Besides being the best way to pay for your items on iPads, it also stores different passes such as hotel links, flight tickets, etc. These Passes, however, need to be discarded after use. To remove a used pass, follow the steps below.

- Open the wallet app.
- Tap on your card, and your passes are displayed at the bottom.
- Tap on the pass
- Tap on the "i" option at the bottom right.
- Scroll down and tap on "Remove Pass."
- This will automatically remove it from the App.

Transferring folders and photos from SD Card

- Connect your iPad Pro with USB-C to SD
- Go to "Photo Album."
- Tap on "Import" at the bottom-right corner of the screen
- Select the photos and files you want to transfer to your iPad
- Tap on "Import" at the top-right corner of your screen
- Tap on "Import Selected"

- You can then go to your photo gallery to view the imported photos.

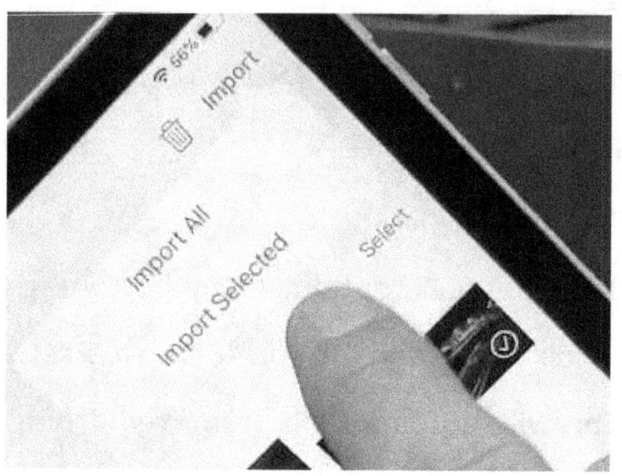

Chapter Seven

Troubleshooting Common Problems

iPad Won't Turn ON

When a device like an iPad Pro wouldn't turn ON or restart, there are always a couple of possibilities. It could be firmware or hardware issues. What you can do is rule out the possibility that it is a matter of firmware problem. The first solution, perform a force restart on the device. Most of the time, when a device like iPad powers down on its own and will no longer restart or turn ON, it's due to a firmware crash. To perform a force restart,

- Press and release the volume up button
- And then, the volume down button.
- Press and hold the power button for about 10 seconds, and the device is forced to build-up
- When the Apple logo appears, release the power button and wait until the iPad finishes reboot.

The second solution, charge, and perform the force restart. The battery may have drained, and the firmware crash just before the device powered off. That might be the reason why it is not responding. Here is what to do,

- Plug the charger to a working wire outlet

- Connect the iPad to it using the original lightning cable

- Regardless of whether the iPad shows charging or not, leave it connected to the charger for at least 10 minutes.

- After a few minutes of charging, while the iPad is connected to the charger, perform a force restart again. If you can get the Apple logo appears on the screen, then the problem has been fixed. But if the iPad still does not turn on after the solutions above, you have to perform DFU Restore, the last resort to fix any software issue on the iPad. To carry out DFU Restore on your iPad Pro 4th Generation, follow the steps below.

- Connect your iPad Pro with iTunes SystemSystem running with an updated version of iPad and connected to the internet

- Quickly press the volume up button, followed by the volume down button.

- Press and hold the power button for about 10 seconds

- While you hold down the power button, press and hold the volume down button for about 5 seconds

- Release the power button while you hold down the volume down button until the iPad pro information appears on the System

- Go to recovery mode if you have to back up your data in iCloud.

- Your iPad Pro will exit recovery mode after about 5o minutes. If you want to exit recovery mode immediately, then perform a force restart on the iPad Pro. If the problem persists after these series of troubleshooting, it could mean the problem is hardware-related.

Frozen iPad Screen

If your iPad pro freezes, it might be due to software malfunction. To unfreeze your device, reboot the device by,

- Quickly press on the volume up button.

- volume down button

- Press and hold the power button until the Apple logo appears.

- iPad Won't charge

If you're your iPad doesn't charge, the problem could be a software or hardware issue. It is good that you start the troubleshooting from the software.

The first solution, perform a force restart on the device. Most of the time, when a device like an iPad fails to charge, it's due to a software crash.

If the force restart does not work, the second solution is to look at the iPad lightning cable for frames and discoloration. Try and charge it with a different lightning cable.

If the solutions above do not work, clean up the lightning port with a soft toothbrush dipped into the methylated spirit.

Apple Pencil Won't write properly.

If the Apple pencil is not working with your iPad Pro, check whether the Apple pencil Bluetooth is turned on or not. To turn on the Bluetooth,

- Place the Apple pencil on top of the magnet
- Tap on the pop-up message "tap to connect."

The Bluetooth will be turned on automatically.

Secondly, if your Apple Pencil doesn't have sufficient charge, it wouldn't write. To charge the Apple pencil, put it on the side of the iPad pro. It will stick to the device and start charging. Please wait until it charges completely.

Your Apple pencil will not write if the tip of the pencil is loose. So, ensure that the tip is properly tightened.

If you forget the Apple pencil, then you reconnect it. To do this, follow the steps below.

- Open Settings
- Scroll down, and tap on "Bluetooth."
- Tap on the "I" icon beside the Apple pencil
- Tap on "Forget this Device."
- Tap on "Forget Device."

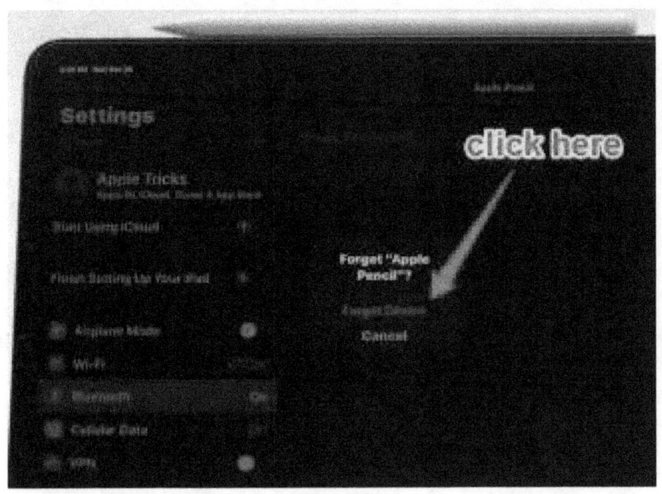

Smart Keyboard won't respond

When the smart keyboard fails to respond, the users find it difficult to type text on the iPad, mostly when the keypad isn't sitting properly on the smart connector, thereby preventing the terminals of the keyboard from making proper contact with the iPad.

To resolve this issue, slide the keyboard either way, and the virtual keyboard will disappear from the screen.

iPad Screen won't rotate

Your iPad screen won't rotate mostly because the device orientation lock is turned ON. To turn OFF the orientation of the iPad, follow the steps below.

- Swipe down the top-right corner of your screen to access the control center

- Locate the device orientation lock button

- Tap the button to turn OFF the orientation lock

- Meanwhile,   if the   device orientation   lock is turned OFF, and the iPad fails to rotate, then the device orientation App has crashed and needs to be closed. To close the orientation App,

- Go to "Settings."

- Scroll down and tap on "General."

- Scroll down to Reset and tap on "Reset All."

- Enter your passcode

- Reconfigure the wi-fi setting after resetting. This should